Sex

Floating
Things

About Starters Science books

STARTERS SCIENCE books are designed to encourage scientific awareness in young children. The series aims to focus the instinctive curiosity of children and to encourage exploration and experiment. It also aims to develop language, encourage discussion and suggest situations where children can examine similarities and differences.

The text of each book is simple enough for children to read for themselves, and the vocabulary has been controlled to ensure that about 90 per cent of the words used will be familiar to them. Each book also contains a picture index and a page of notes for parents and teachers.

Written and planned by Albert James
Illustrator: Margaret Theakston

A MACDONALD BOOK

© Macdonald & Co (Publishers) Ltd 1973

First published in
Great Britain in 1973

Reprinted 1974, 1983 and 1986

Printed and bound in Great Britain by
Hazell, Watson & Viney Ltd
Aylesbury, Buckinghamshire

Published by Macdonald & Co (Publishers) Ltd
Greater London House
Hampstead Road
London NW1 7QX

Members of BPCC plc

British Library Cataloguing in Publication Data
James, Albert
Floating things. — (Starters science)
  1. Readers — 1950 —
  I. Title II. Series
  428.6   PE1119

  ISBN 0-356-04823-3
  ISBN 0-356-09282-8 Pbk

STARTERS
SCIENCE

Floating
Things

Macdonald

What can you see floating on this pond?

2

There are ducks and swans on the river.
What else can you see on the water?

Lots of things float on the sea.
How many floating things can you count
in the picture?
Can you think of any more?

4

lifebelt

lifejacket

These people are in a sailing boat.
Why do they wear lifejackets?
What is the lifebelt for?

Here are some small boats.
There are many different kinds.
What kinds have you seen?
6

Some boats have motors.
In what other ways
are boats moved along?

These are all big ships.
They float on the sea.

8

Which ship is an aircraft-carrier?
Can you see a trawler?

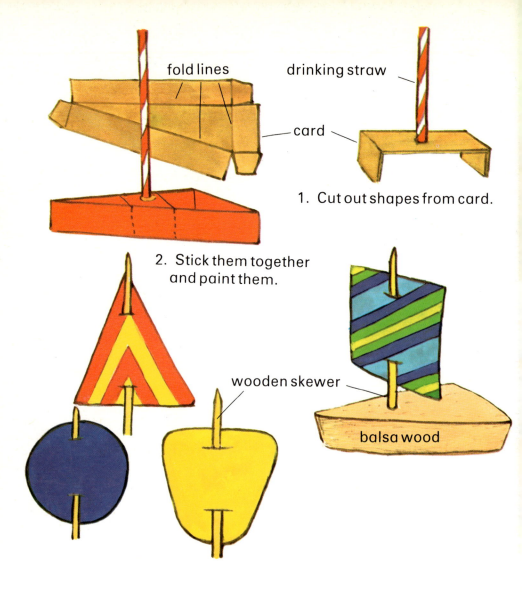

fold lines

drinking straw

card

1. Cut out shapes from card.

2. Stick them together and paint them.

wooden skewer

balsa wood

You can make model boats like these.
Use card or balsa wood.
Blow on the sails to make them move.

10

elastic band

card

wood

You can make this paddle-boat.
Wind it up and let it go.
How far does it travel?

Try some different boat shapes.
Give each a gentle push.
Which shape goes the best?

12

Some things float on water.
Others sink to the bottom.
Try some out and see.

These tree trunks have come from the forest.
They float down the river to the saw-mill.
Men make sure the logs keep moving.
They jump from log to log.

14

Try floating a block of wood.
Float some different kinds of wood
beside it.
Is there any difference?

Ice floats.
Float an ice-cube in a glass bowl.
Is more ice under the water or above it?

16

Icebergs float in the sea.
They are dangerous to ships.

Try to push a polystyrene block
under water.
Do you have to push hard?
18

Try to lift two bricks.
Lift one in water.
Can you feel any difference?

19

modelling clay

A ball of modelling clay sinks.
Press it into a hollow shape.
Then it will float.
Can it carry any cargo?
20

Knives, forks and spoons all sink.
Bottles, lids and saucepans can float.
Hollow shapes can float.

21

Float two empty jars in water.
How much sand can you put in one
before it sinks?
How much water in the other?
22

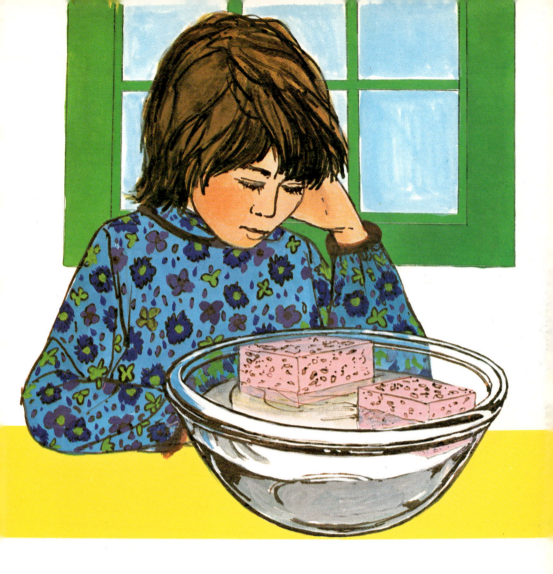

The air holes in a sponge make it float
high out of the water.
Squeeze it to fill the holes with water.
How does it float now?

You can make a bubbly-can.
Hold it down in the water.
What do you hear?
What do you see?
24

Put one end of a tube into the can
and blow down it.
Does this bring the can to the top again?

tanks

This is a submarine.
Water is let into tanks to make it sink.
The water is blown out again
to make the submarine rise.
26

milk

cooking oil

salt

water-line mark

paper clips

Make some floats with drinking straws.
Mark the line of the water.
Now try them in salt water.
Try them in milk and cooking oil.

Index

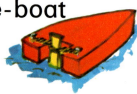

Notes for Parents and Teachers

Starters Science books are designed for children to read and study on their own, but children would also benefit by sharing these topics with a parent or teacher. These brief notes explain the scientific ideas contained in the book, and help the interested adult to expand the themes.

2–4   Illustrations of water scenes in which children can identify animals and plant life found floating on the surface. They can also relate these observations to the various boats and toys.

5   An introduction to lifebelts and lifejackets.

6–9   Children are encouraged to observe and find out about different kinds of boats and how they are propelled.

10–12 Children are shown how to construct some simple model sailing boats as well as a paddle boat that really works. They can investigate different boat shapes to find the ones that work best.

13–19 A series of experiments and observations concerning buoyancy. Children discover that different kinds of wood float with different amounts below the water level, and that some may not float at all. They can learn about icebergs and experiment with ice-cubes.

20–23 These experiments will help children to experience that hollow shaped objects will often float, while solid masses of the same material will sink. Children can discover that when the airholes in a sponge are filled with water, its buoyancy is greatly reduced.

24–25 Projects for fun—making bubbly-cans.

26   A detailed cut-away illustration of a submarine to show how increasing the amount of air in its tanks will make it surface.

27   Fun with floats—leading to the discovery that a weighted drinking straw will float at different heights in different liquids.